I0795718

Cheryl Frances-Hoad

Punjabi Proverbs

for mezzo-soprano, baritone and piano

(2024)

Chester Music

Commissioned by the Leeds Lieder Festival with generous support from Peter Hirschmann, Martin Staniforth and The Marchus Trust

First performed on 16 April 2024 as part of the Leeds Lieder Festival at Sikh Centre, Leeds, UK by Nina Kanter (soprano), Oscar Castellino (baritone) and Keval Shah (piano).

Duration: *c.* 12 minutes

Order No. **CH88373**
EAN 5020679008201

Published by
Chester Music Limited
14-15 Berners Street, London W1T 3LJ
Tel. +44 (0)20 7612 7400

Exclusive Distributors:
Hal Leonard Europe Limited
42 Wigmore Street, London W1U 2RN
Tel. +44 (0)20 7395 0380

www.wisemusicclassical.com
e-mail: promotion@wisemusic.com

COMPOSER'S NOTE

Punjabi Proverbs was premiered at The Sikh Centre, Leeds on 16th April 2024 as part of the Leeds Lieder Festival by Nina Kanter, soprano, Oscar Castellino, baritone, and Keval Shah, piano. The nine short songs set a collection of Punjabi proverbs and aphorisms in a series of solos and duos. The concert (co-promoted by South Asian Arts UK and curated by Keval Shah) celebrated the fusion of Western and Indian classical arts, and included settings by British and diaspora Indian composers of poetry written by, among others, Kabir, Mirabai and Tagore.

Cheryl Frances-Hoad

TEXT

Gurmukhī

੧. ਤੁਰਿਆ ਤੇ ਅੱਪੜਿਯਾ
ਪਰਾਈ ਆਸ, ਆਈ ਨਾ ਰਾਸ
ਆਪ ਬੁਰੇ ਤਾਂ ਜੱਗ ਬੁਰਾ, ਆਪ ਭਲੇ ਤਾਂ ਜੱਗ ਭਲਾ
ਸੱਜਣ ਉਹੋ ਜਿਹੜਾ ਮੂੰਹ ਤੇ ਸੱਚ ਆਖੇ
ਆਸਾ ਜੀਏ ਨਿਰਾਸਾ ਮਰੇ

੨. ਨਿੰਉ ਨ ਲੱਗਦਾ ਜੋੜੀ ਦਾ
ਨੈਣ ਮਿਲਾ ਕੇ ਕਦੇ ਚੈਨ ਨਹੀਂ ਮਿਲਦਾ
ਰਖਿਏ ਤੇ ਪ੍ਰੀਤ, ਨਹੀਂ ਤੇ ਪਲੀਤ

੩. ਮੂੰਹ ਦੀ ਬੱਲੇ ਬੱਲੇ, ਤੇ ਹੱਥਾਂ ਦੀ ਹੜਤਾਲ
ਕਰਤੂਤ ਨ ਕੋਈ ਪੱਲੇ, ਕਰਨੀ ਬੱਲੇ ਬੱਲੇ
ਰੱਬ ਨੇੜੇ ਕੇ ਘਸੁੰਨ
ਜਿਹਦੀ ਬਾਂਦਰੀ ਉਹੀ ਨਚਾਵੇ
ਕੋਠੇ ਤੋਂ ਡਿੱਗ ਪਈ, ਵੇਹੜੇ ਨਾਲ ਰੁੱਸ ਪਈ
ਆ ਕਰ ਫੂੰ, ਤੇ ਫਿਟੇ ਮੂੰਹ

੪. ਕੋਠੀ ਵਾਲਾ ਰੋਵੇ, ਛੱਪਰ ਵਾਲਾ ਸੋਵੇ
ਰਾਂਝਾ, ਸਭ ਦਾ ਸਾਂਝਾ

੫. ਵੇਲੇ ਦੀ ਨਮਾਜ਼, ਕੁਵੇਲੇ ਦਿਆਂ ਟੱਕਰਾਂ
ਗੌਣਾ ਤੇ ਰੋਣਾ ਸਭ ਨੂੰ ਅਓਂਦਾ ਏ

੬. ਇੱਕ ਇੱਕਲਾਪਾ, ਸੌ ਸਿਆਪਾ
ਆਸਾ ਜੀਏ, ਨਿਰਾਸਾ ਮਰੇ

੭. ਪੱਲੇ ਨਈ ਧੇਲਾ, ਕਰਦੀ ਮੇਲਾ ਮੇਲਾ
ਪੈਸਾ ਓਹਦਾ, ਜਿਦੇ ਪੱਲੇ
ਰੱਬ ਵੀ ਭਰਿਆਂ ਨੂੰ ਹੀ ਭਰਦਾ ਏ
ਪੈਸੇ ਵਾਲੀ ਦਾ ਹੀ ਬਾਲ ਖੇਡੇ

੮. ਪਾਵੇ ਹਰ ਕੋਈ, ਠਮਕਾਵੇ ਕੋਈ ਕੋਈ
ਆਸਾ ਜੀਏ, ਨਿਰਾਸਾ ਮਰੇ

੯. ਜੇਹੜਾ ਸੁੱਖ ਛੱਜੂ ਦੇ ਚੋਬਾਰੇ, ਉਹ ਬਲਖ ਨ ਬੁਖਾਰੇ
ਆਸਾ ਜੀਏ, ਨਿਰਾਸਾ ਮਰੇ

A recording of the spoken Punjabi (with thanks to Harpreet Kaur Sagoo) can be accessed by scanning the QR code below:

Transliteration

IPA

English

1.
Turreya te apparreya.
Parayi aas, aayi na raas.
Aap bure taañ jag bura, aap bhale taañ jag bhala.
Sajjan uho jehra munh te sach aakhe.
Aasa jiye, nirasa mare.

[tuɽəja] [ʈe] [apaɽəja]
[pəɽa:j] [a:s] [a:j] [na] [ɽa:s]
[a:pə] [buɽe:] [tã] [dʒagə] [buɽa:] [a:pə] [bəle:] [tã] [dʒagə] [bəla:]
[saɟãn] [o] [ɟe:ɽa] [mṵn] [te:] [sac] [akʰe]
[a:sa] [ɟijɛ] [ni:ɽasa] [maɽe:]

You will get there, provided you start.
Expectations lead to disappointments.
Be good and people will be good to you. Be bad and expect the same.
A friend is one who speaks truth to your face.
Hope keeps you alive.

2.
Neoñh na lagda jori da.
Nain mila ke kade chain nai milda.
Rakhiye te preet, nahi te paleet.

[nɔ̰] [nə] [lagda] [ɟɔɽi] [da]
[nɛ̰nə] [məla] [ke] [kɑɖe] [cɛ̰] [ni] [miɭɖa]
[ɽɑkʰijɛ] [te] [pɽitə] [nɛhi] [te] [plitə]

You can't make yourself fall in love.
Fall in love, embrace restlessness.
It's love if you sustain it, lust otherwise.

3.
Muh di ballay ballay te hathan di harrtaal!
Kartoot na koi palle, karni balle balle!
Rab nede me ghassun?
Jiddi baandari ohi nachave.
Kothe ton digg payi, vehrre naal russ payi.
Aakar phoon te fitte mu!

[mu] [di] [baɭe] [baɭe] [te] [haʈʰã] [di] [haɽtaɭ]
[kaɽʈoʈə] [na] [kɔj] [paɭɛ] [kaɳi] [baɭe] [baɭe]
[ɽabə] [nede] [mi] [gasun]
[ɟɛɖi] [bãːndɾi] [ɔhi] [nacʰave]
[kɔtʰe] [tɔ̰] [dɪgə] [pɛɪ] [veɾe] [naɭ] [ɽuspɛɪ]
[aːkəɽ][pʰõ] [ʈɛ] [fɪʈɛ] [mu]

All talk and no action!
Got nothing to show for it but boasting all the time!
What's closer, God or my punch?
Not my circus, not my monkeys.
Fallen off the roof but pissed at the courtyard.
Nobody welcomes an arrogant bastard!

4.
Kothi wala roway, chhappar wala soway.
Ranjha, sub da sanjha.

[kotʰi] [waɭa] [ɽowe] [cʰapaɽə] [waɭa] [sowe]
[ɽaɲɟʰɑ] [sɤb] [da] [saɲɟʰa]

The rich are restless, the poor sleep peacefully.
It's the same God everyone looks up to.

5.
Vele di namaz, kavele dian takkran.
Gana te rona sabh nu aaunda ae.

[weːle] [di] [nəmaz] [kəwele] [dija] [takɽã]
[gãɳã] [te] [ɽõna] [sabə] [nu] [ɔ̰ndaɪ]

Some things are best done in their proper time.
You'll sing and you'll cry. That is human.

6.
Ik iklaapa, sau siyapa.
Aasa jiye, nirasa mare.

[ɪk’] [əlapa] [soː] [sijapa]
[aːsa] [ɟiɽe] [niɽasa] [maɽe]

Loneliness is the cause of a hundred issues.
Hope keeps you alive.

7.
Palle nai dhela, kardi mela mela?
Paisa ohda, jihde pallay.
Rab vi bhareyan nu hi bharda ae.
Paisay wali da ee baal khede.

[pale] [ne] [d̥elɑʔ] [kaɽɖi] [meɭa] [meɭa]
[pɛːsa] [ʔoda] [ɟiɖɛ] [palɛɪ]
[ɽab̥ə] [wi] [b̥aɽeja] [nu] [b̥aɽɖaɪ]
[pɛːsi] [waɭi] [dɑ] [baɭ] [kʰede]

Got no money but want to go shopping, eh?
Money works for those who own it.
Only the rich get richer.
A rich woman’s boy can play.

8.
Paawe har koi, thamkawe koi.
Aasa jiye, nirasa mare.

[paːwe] [haɽ] [kɔɪ] [tʰəməkave] [kɔɪ]
[aːsa] [ɟije] [nirasa] [maɽe]

Every woman wears anklets, but only some can make them tinkle.
Hope keeps you alive.

9.
Jehra sukh chhaju de chobare, oh balakh na bukhare.
Aasa jiye, nirasa mare.

[ɟeɽa] [sukʰ] [cʰaɟu] [de] [cʰəbaɽe] [o] [baɭkʰə] [na] [bukʰaɽe]
[aːsa] [ɟije] [niɽasa] [maɽeː]

East or west, home is best.
Hope keeps you alive.

Punjabi Proverbs

Traditional

CHERYL FRANCES-HOAD

1.

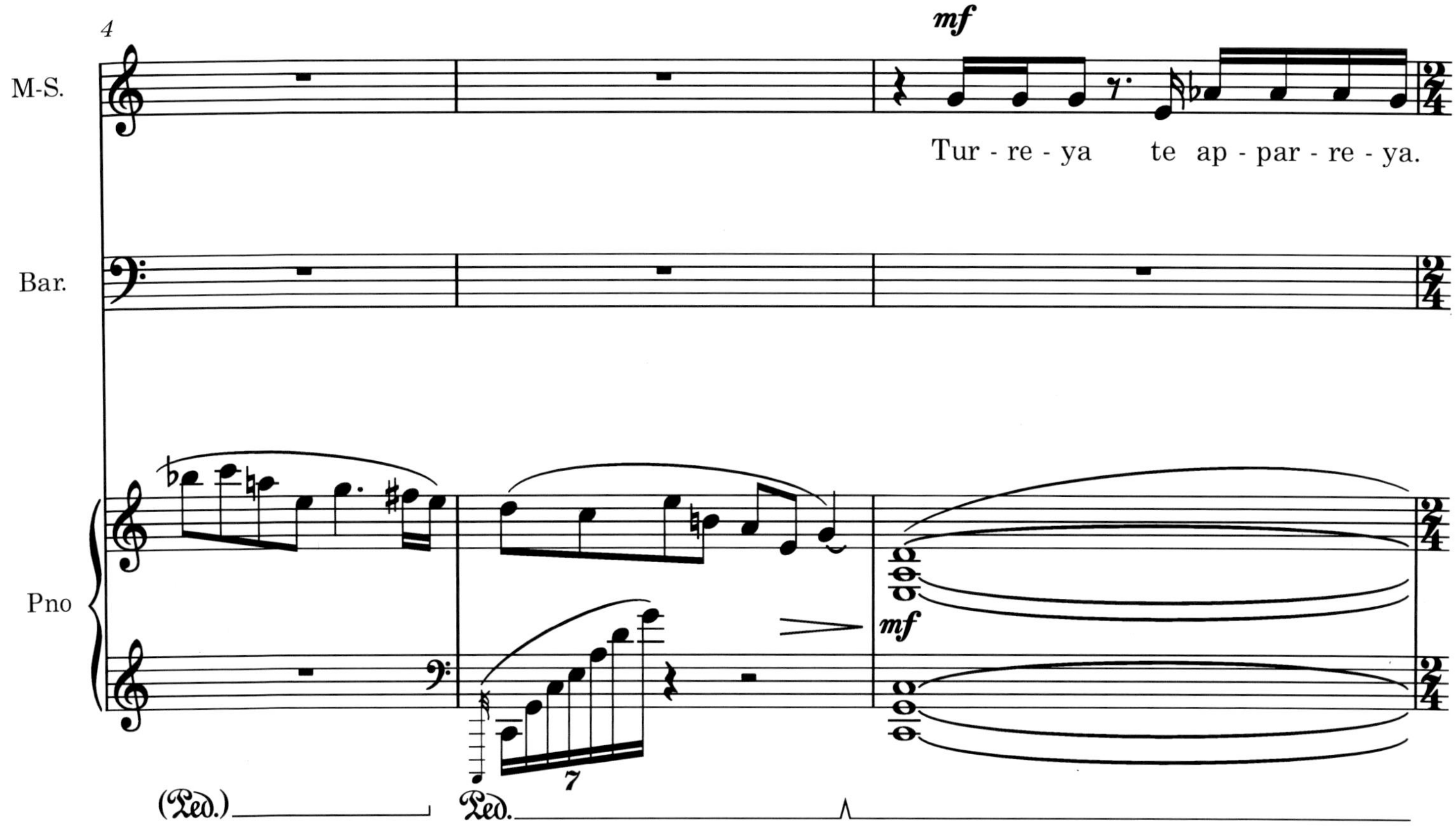

7
M-S.
Bar.
mf
3
Pa - ra - yi aas, aa - yi na raas.
Pno
(Ped.)
8ba
10
M-S.
3
Aa - p bu - re taañ jag bu - ra,
Bar.
Pno

11
M-S.
Bar.
aa - p bha - le taañ jag bha - la.
3
Pno
3
3
8ba
A
12
M-S.
Saj - jan u - ho jeh - ra
Bar.
Pno
11
f
Ped.

13
poco rit.
M-S.
munh te sach aa - khe.
Bar.
Saj - jan u - ho jeh - ra
munh te sach aa - khe.
Pno
mf
(Ped.)
a tempo
15
mp
Aa - sa ji - ye, ni - ra - sa ma - re.
Aa - sa ji - ye, ni - ra - sa ma - re.
8va
5
Ped.

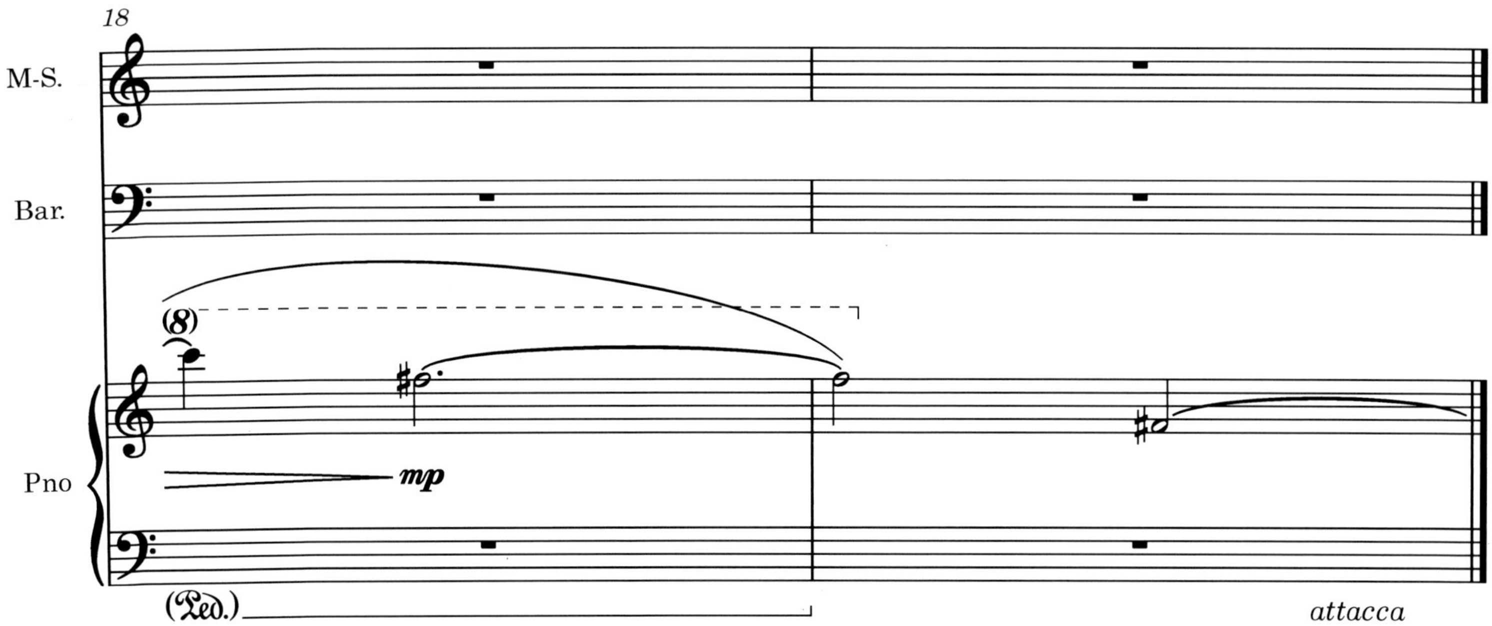
18
M-S.
Bar.
(8)
mp
Pno
(Ped.)
attacca

2.

Andante cantabile (♩ = c. 88)
Piano
(mp)
poco
con pedal
4
Pno
poco
poco
7
Pno
mf
simile

9
Pno
mp
12
mp
M-S.
Neoñh na lag - da jo - ri da,
Pno
poco
15
M-S.
neoñh na lag - - - -
Pno
poco

18
mf
mp
poco
M-S.
- - - - - - da jo - - ri da,
Pno
mf
mp
poco
20
poco
M-S.
Pno
poco
B
24
mp
M-S.
neoñh na lag - da jo - ri da.
mp
Bar.
Nain mi - la ke ka - de chai - n nai mil - da,
Pno

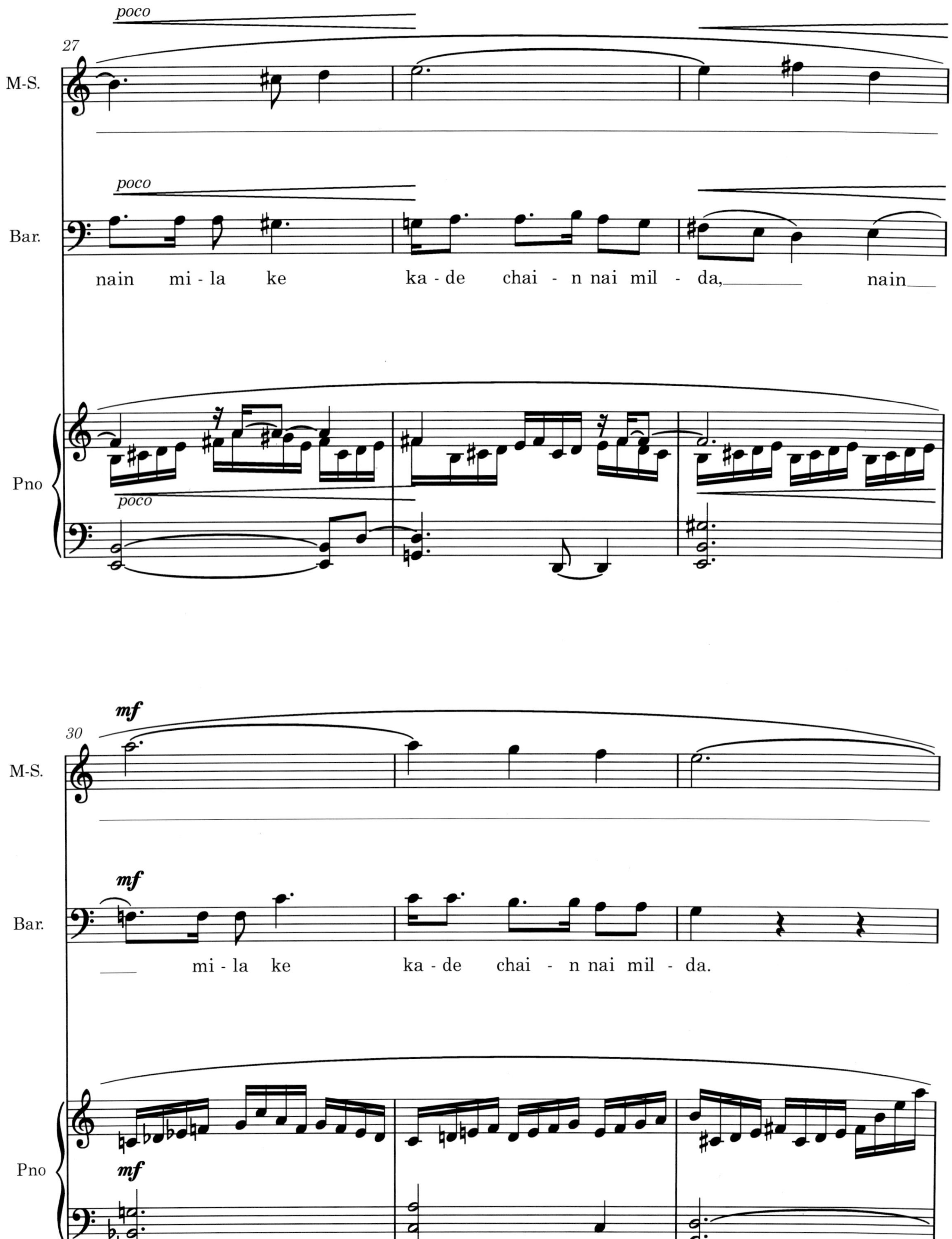
poco
27
M-S.
poco
Bar.
nain mi - la ke ka - de chai - n nai mil - da, nain
Pno
poco
mf
30
M-S.
mf
Bar.
mi - la ke ka - de chai - n nai mil - da.
Pno
mf

C
poco rit.
33
M-S.
Bar.
Pno
meno f
mp
Ra - khi - ye te preet, na - hi te pa - leet.
Ra - khi - ye te preet, na - hi te pa - leet.
poco
37
a tempo
Neoñh na lag - da
p
mp
poco

40
M-S.
jo - ri da.
Bar.
Neoñh na
Pno
poco

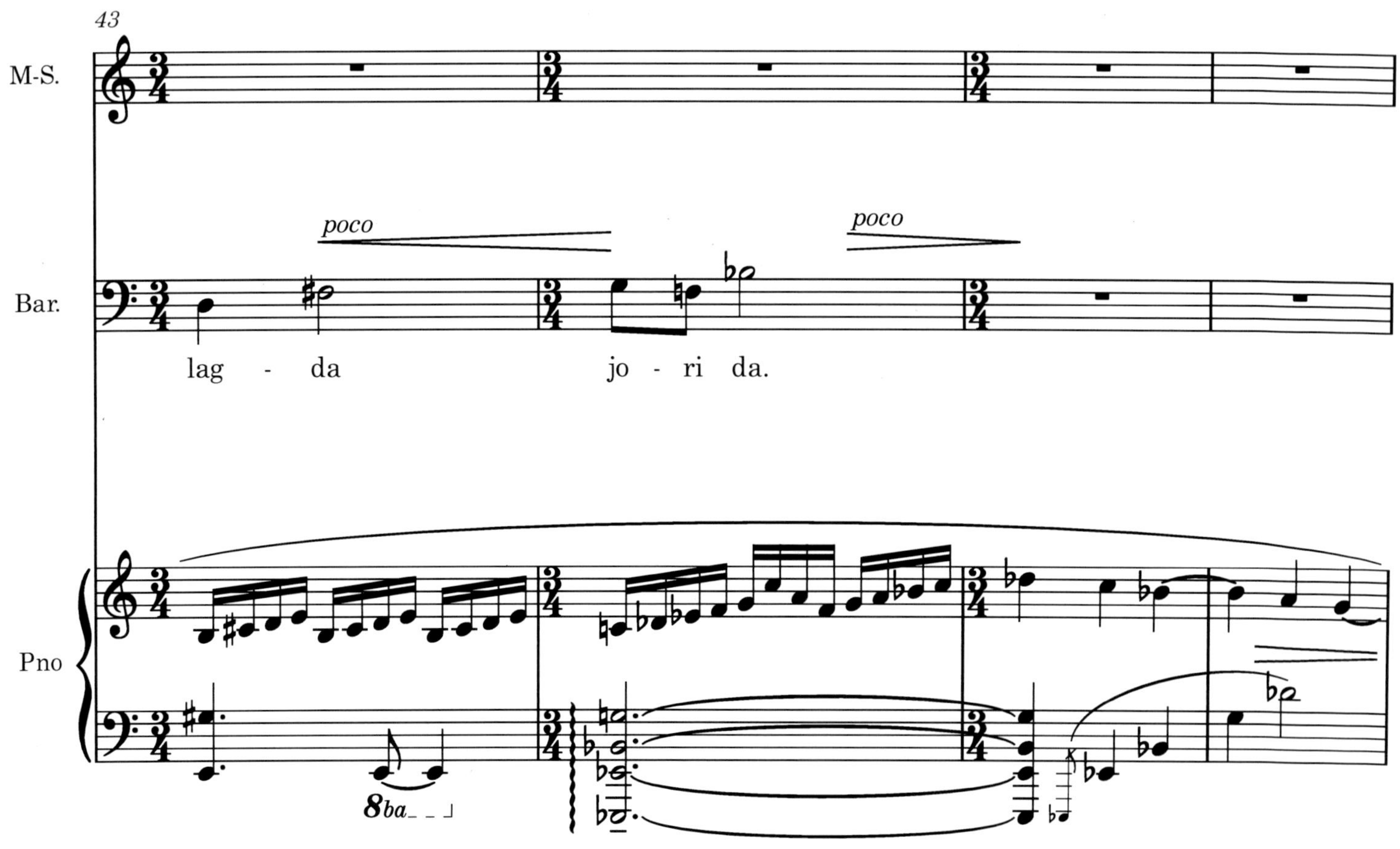
43
M-S.
poco
poco
Bar.
lag - da jo - ri da.
Pno
8ba

D
Pno
mp
poco
8ba
Poco meno mosso
M-S.
Nain mi - la ke ka - de chai - n nai mil - da.
Bar.
Nain mi - la ke ka - de chai - n nai mil - da.
Pno
p

3.

Allegro scherzando (♩= c. 132)
Piano
mf
4
Pno
poco
mf
7
Pno
f
11
M-S.
mf
Muh di bal - lay bal - lay te ha - than di harr - taal!
Bar.
mf
Kar-
Pno
mf
poco

14
M-S.
Bar.
Pno
poco
-too - t na koi pal - le, kar - ni bal - le bal - le!
mf
poco
18
f
E
Ra - b ne - de me ghas - sun?
mf
Jid - di baan - d'ri
f
mf
22
mf
Ko - the ton dig - g pa - yi, vehr - re
3
o - hi na - cha - ve.

25
M-S.
naa - l russ pa - yi.
Pno
3
mp
28
Pno
f
31
M-S.
f
Aa - kar phoon te fit - te mu!
f
Bar.
Aa - kar phoon te fit - te mu!
Pno
ff

4.

Larghetto solenne (♩ = c. 60)
poco
poco
Piano
mp
Bar.
Pno
mp
Ko - thi wa - la
ro - way, chhap - par wa - la so - way, ko -
poco
poco
poco

9
Bar.
thi wa - la ro - way, chhap - par wa - - - - la
poco
poco
poco
poco
Pno
F
12
mp
M-S.
Ran - jha, sub da
Bar.
so - way, ko - - - - - - - - - - -
poco
Pno
14
M-S.
san jha, ran - jha,
Bar.
thi wa - - - - - - - - la
poco
Pno

16
M-S.
sub da san - - jha,
Bar.
ro - - - way, chhap - par wa - - - - - -
poco
Pno
18
cresc. poco a poco
M-S.
ran - jha, sub da
cresc. poco a poco
Bar.
- - - - - - - - - la so - - -
poco
poco
Pno
cresc. poco a poco

G
20
M-S.
san - jha, ran - - jha, sub da
Bar.
- way, ko - thi wa - - - la ro - - - - -
Pno
22
M-S.
san - - jha, ran - jha, sub da
Bar.
- - way, chhap - par wa - la so - - way,
Pno

25
M-S.
Bar.
Pno
(mf)
poco
san - - - - - - - - - - - - jha.
ko - - - - - thi wa - la ro - - - - - -
28
H
mp
- way, chhap - par wa - la so - way.

31
M-S.
Bar.
Pno
Ran - jha, sub da san - jha.
p
poco
33
Pno
p

5.

Moderato affabile ♩ = 112
Piano
mp
poco
poco
4
Pno
poco
poco
6
I
M-S.
mp
poco
Ga - na te
Bar.
mp
Ve - le di na - maz, ka - ve - le di - an tak - k - ran.
Pno
poco
poco
poco

poco
9
M-S.
ro - - - - - na
sabh nu
Pno
poco
poco rit.
12
aaun - - - - - - - - - - - da ae,
Rubato
mf
15
ga - - - - - - - - na te ro - - - -
18
- na sabh nu aaun - - - - - da ae.
mp

23
J
a tempo
(mp)
Bar.
Ve - le di na - maz, ka -
Pno
(mp)
poco
poco
26
Bar.
- ve - le di - an tak - k - ran.
Pno
poco
poco
mf
p

6.

Largo (♩ = c. 40)
Mezzo-soprano
Baritone
Piano
mp dolente
mf
Ik ik - laa - pa,_ sau si - ya - pa.
(non-arpeggio)
mf
4
mp dolce
M-S.
Aa - sa ji - ye,_ ni - ra - sa ma - re.
Bar.
Pno
mp
p

7.

Allegro moderato (♩ = c. 120)
Piano
mf scherzando
mp
mf
5
Bar.
Pno
mf
Pal - le nai dhe - la,
9
M-S.
Pai - sa oh - da,
kar - di me - la me - la?
f

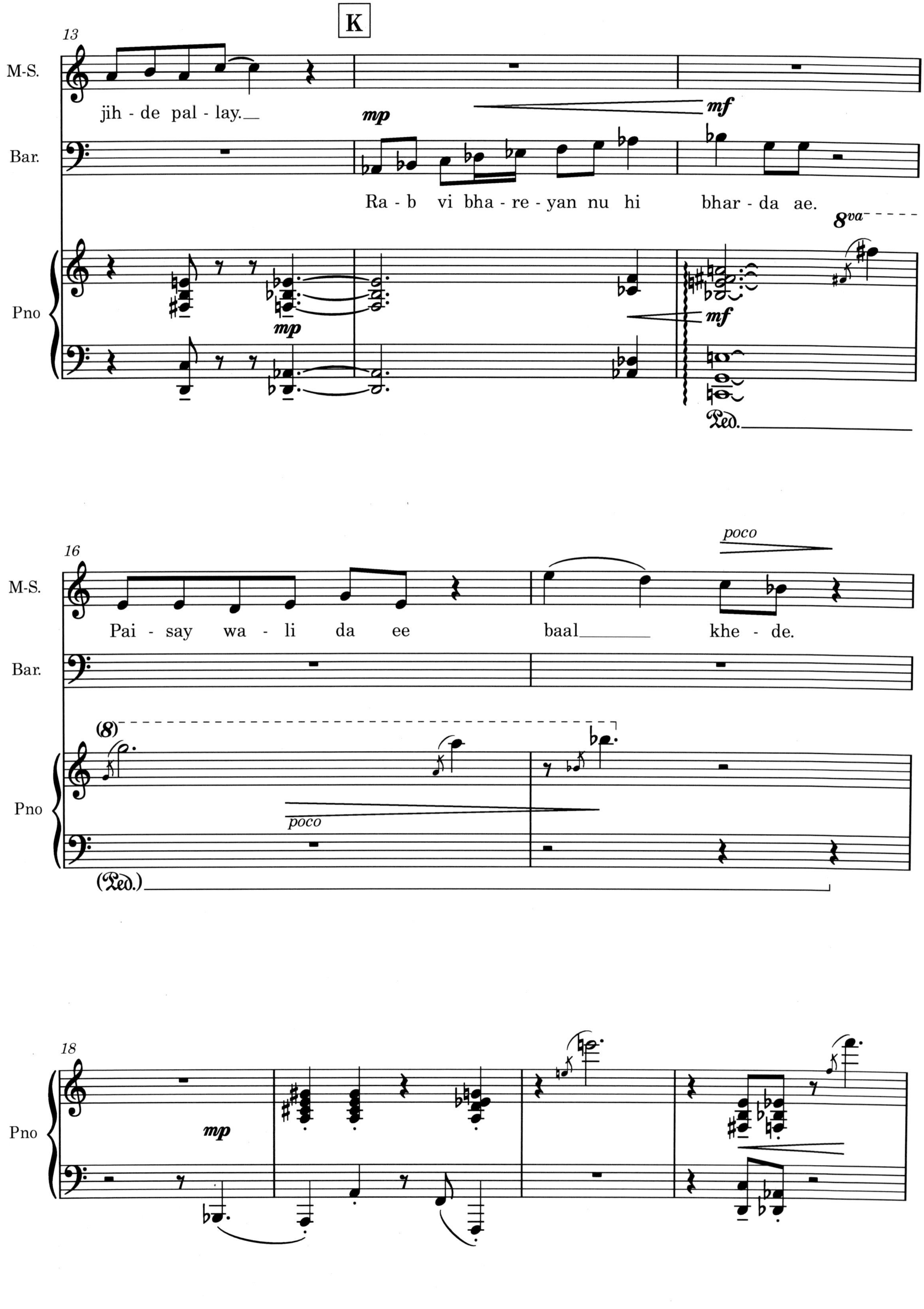
K
13
M-S.
jih - de pal - lay.
Bar.
mp
mf
Ra - b vi bha - re - yan nu hi bhar - da ae.
8va
Pno
mp
mf
Ped.
16
M-S.
Pai - say wa - li da ee baal khe - de.
poco
Bar.
(8)
Pno
poco
(Ped.)
18
Pno
mp

L
22
poco
Bar.
Pal - le nai dhe - la, kar - di mc - la me - la?
8va
Pno
mf
più f
f
8ba
25
mf
M-S.
Pai - sa oh - da,
Bar.
8va
Pno
mf
27
mp
M-S.
jih - de pal - lay, jih - de pal - lay.
Bar.
8va
Pno
mp

8.

Moderato grazioso (♩ = c. 120)
8va
tr
Piano
p
mp
Pno
poco
M
mp cantabile
M-S.
Paa - we har ko - i, tham - ka - we ko - i, paa - -
(8)

21
poco
M-S.
we har ko - i, tham - ka - we
(8)
tr
Pno
poco
26
poco
N
ko - i, paa
30
we har

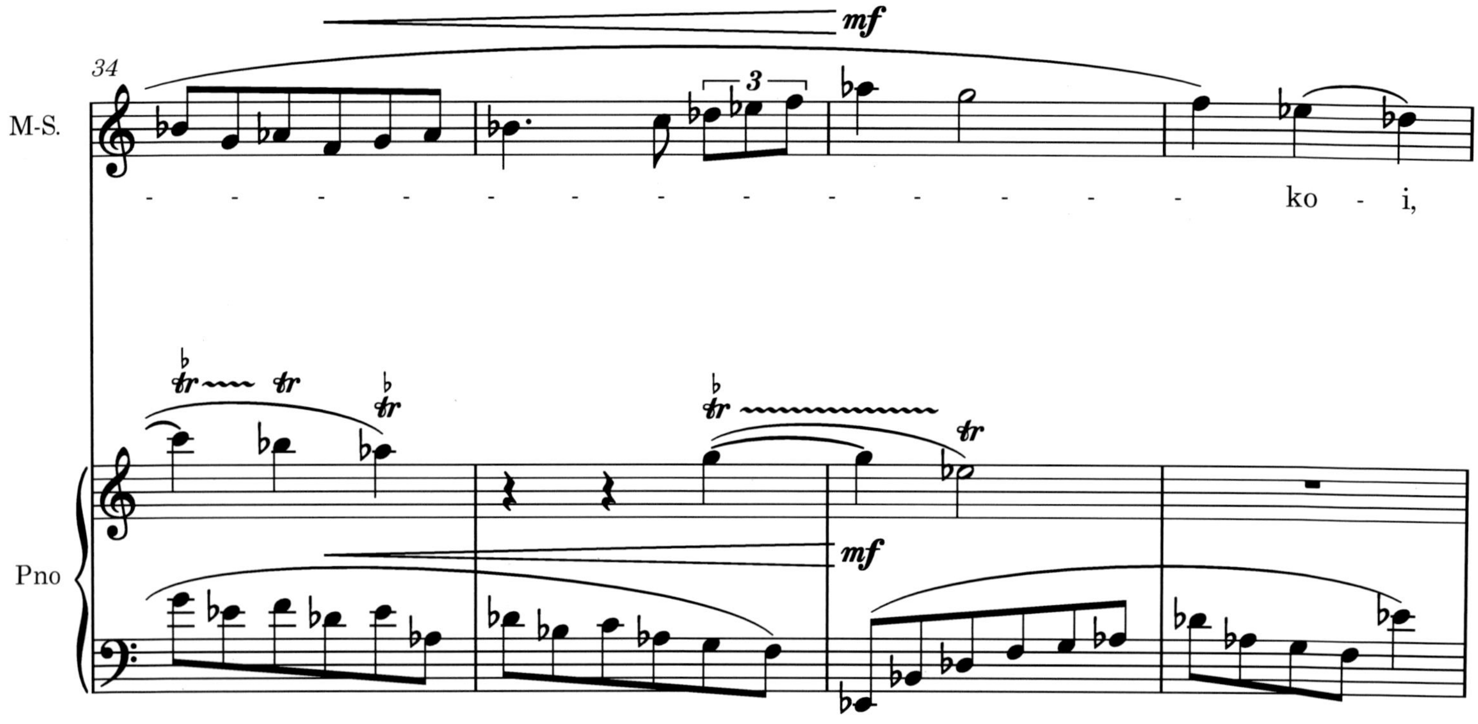
mf
34
M-S.
ko - i,
Pno
mf

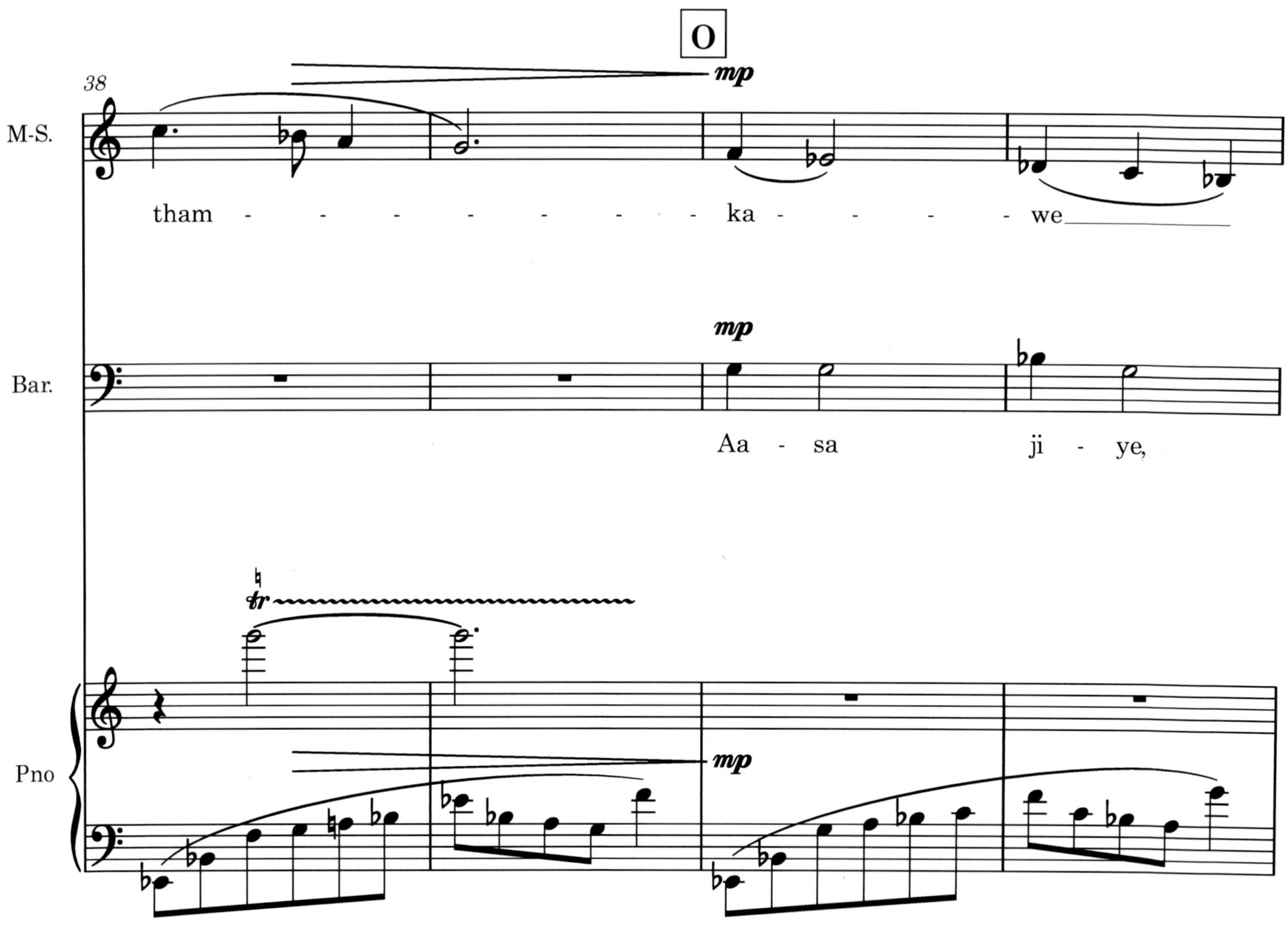
O
mp
38
M-S.
tham - ka - we
mp
Bar.
Aa - sa ji - ye,
Pno
mp

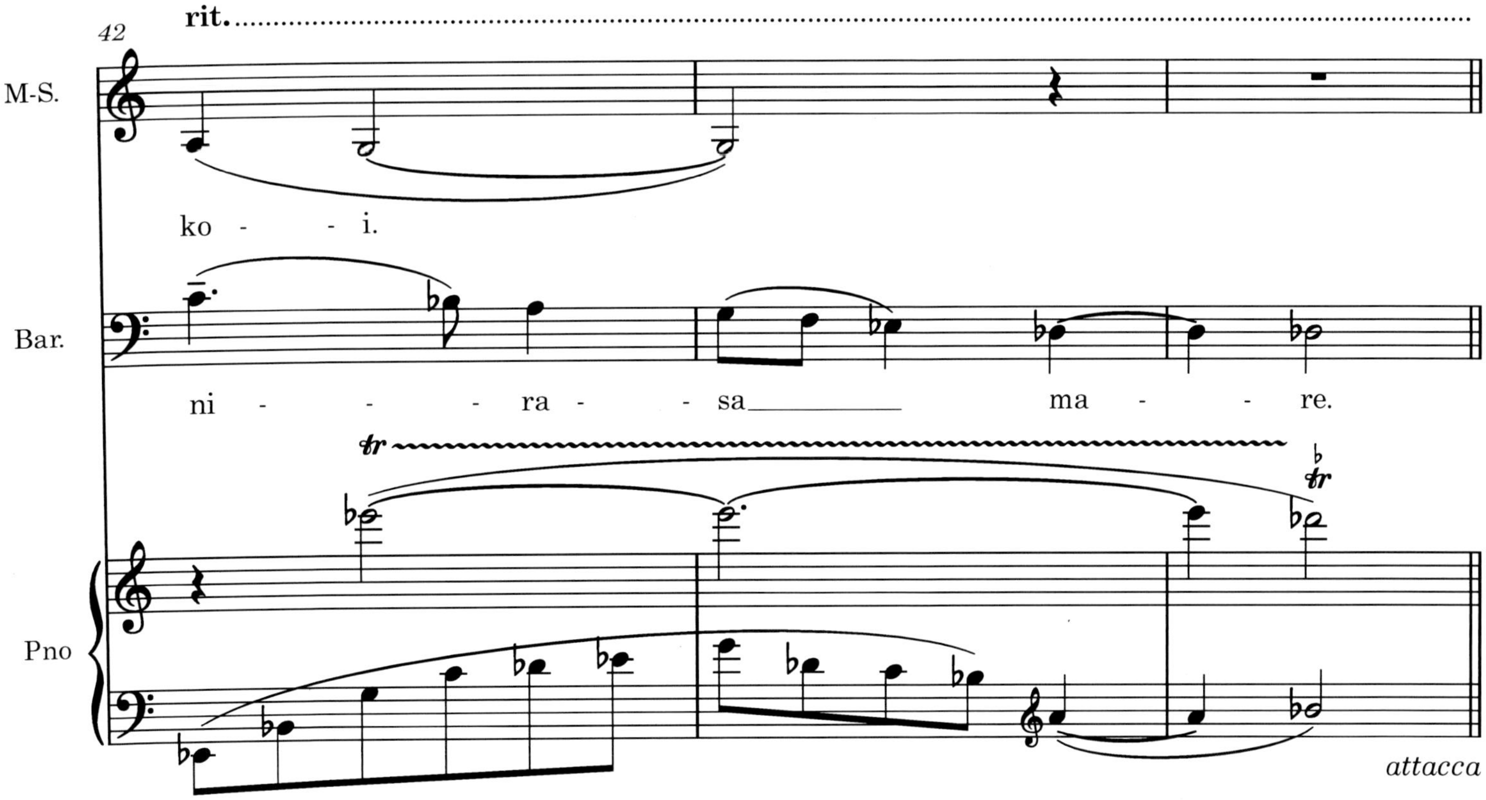
42
rit.
M-S.
ko - - i.
Bar.
ni - - ra - - sa ma - - re.
tr
tr
Pno
attacca

9.

Adagio glorioso (♩ = c. 60)
Mezzo-soprano
mf
Jeh - ra sukh chha - ju de cho - ba - re, oh
Baritone
mf
Jeh - ra sukh chha - ju de cho - ba - re, oh
Piano
mp
mf
Ped.

3
M-S.
più f
ba - lakh na bu - kha - re,__ jeh - ra sukh chha - ju de cho - ba - re, oh
Bar.
più f
ba - lakh na bu - kha - re,__ jeh - ra sukh chha - ju de cho - ba - re, oh
Pno
più f
8va
(Ped.)
Ped.
8ba

P
6
M-S.
f
ba - lakh na bu - kha - re,_ jeh - ra sukh chha - ju de cho - ba - re,__ oh
Bar.
f
ba - lakh na bu - kha - re,_ jeh - ra sukh chha - ju de cho - ba - re,__ oh
Pno
(8)
f
(Ped.)
8ba

9
M-S.
ba - lakh na bu - kha - - - re, oh ba - lakh na bu - kha - - re,
mf
Bar.
ba - lakh na bu - kha - - - re, oh ba - lakh na bu - kha - - re,
mf
Pno
mf
8ba
12
M-S.
jeh - - ra sukh chha - ju de cho - ba - re, oh
Bar.
jeh - - - - ra sukh chha - ju de cho - ba - re, oh
Pno
mp
8ba

Cheryl Frances-Hoad,
February 2024